T0194856

And The House Was *Filled*

The Radical Gift of Sacrifice

DEBBIE VANDERSLICE

WESTBOW
PRESS®
A DIVISION OF THOMAS NELSON
& ZONDERVAN

WestBow Press books may be ordered through booksellers or by contacting:

WestBow Press
A Division of Thomas Nelson & Zondervan
1663 Liberty Drive
Bloomington, IN 47403
www.westbowpress.com
1 (866) 928-1240

Unless noted otherwise, all Scripture quotations are taken from The Holy
Bible, English Standard Version® (ESV®), Copyright © 2001 by Crossway,
a publishing ministry of Good News Publishers. All rights reserved.

Scripture quotations marked NIV are taken from The Holy Bible, New
International Version®, NIV® Copyright © 1973, 1978, 1984, 2011 by
Biblica, Inc.® Used by permission. All rights reserved worldwide.

ISBN: 978-1-9736-7167-1 (sc)
ISBN: 978-1-9736-7166-4 (e)

Print information available on the last page.

WestBow Press rev. date: 08/07/2019

"Then Mary took about a pint of pure nard, an expensive perfume; she poured it on Jesus' feet and wiped his feet with her hair. **And the house was filled** *with the fragrance of the perfume." John 12:3; ESV*

Debbie Vanderslice has taken time from her creative and inspirational writing to work on my Grandfather's letters from WWI. She amazingly transcribed over 100 letters from World War I, deciphering locations in England and France and capturing all the unfamiliar language of that era. Her dedication drove the project. I am so grateful for her energy and drive over these past 3 years. Letters from that time were heavily censored and therefore not too interesting. Debbie was able to persist despite anything new to discover in the content. It was a good project thanks to her excellent work. I've been sharing the letters with my extended family. We are all getting to know my Grandfather's love of France which we all suspected growing up. He spoke French to us, often. Now we know why. I have developed a sense of gratitude for the surgery performed by French doctors in Paris that saved my Grandfather's life. We never would have known about this without Debbie's work.

Louise L. Montgomery

Eight Benefits of Pain and Suffering

Written by Debbie Vanderslice

Suffering and pain are a part of everyone's life. We do so much to avoid it, numb it. Talented writer, Debbie Vanderslice, who knows more about pain than many of us teaches us through her own journey with pain and suffering about the "treasure" she has found in dark times where she was empowered to see God's presence. Her story of faith empowers us to do the same.

The Rev. Dr. Joanna Seibert M D., emeritus professor of Pediatric Radiology, Arkansas Children's Hospital, University of Arkansas Medical Sciences, author and ordained deacon in the Episcopal Church

Dedication

To my Hannah banana
You are the best daughter in the world.
Your love motivates me everyday

To Martha
Your life is ever before me urging me on in this thing called life
I miss you

To Madison and Dane and Jane and Margie
Martha was simply the best

To Sherry and Leigh Anne
Two individuals who have restored my faith in humanity

To:Kay:

For showing me how to hope again in a best friend

To, Louise, Lisa, Ginny, Kathy, Shirley, Ann, Dana, Joanna,

Thanks for your generous support

To: Mom, Cynthia, Chip, Edy, Gibbs, and Shep

For simply showing me what love of family really means

About the Author

Debbie Vanderslice graduated with a B.A. with honors in history from Southern Methodist University in Dallas, Texas, where she played tennis on a full scholarship. With her strong writing skills and love for God, Debbie has gone on to work freelance for such companies as DaySpring, Celebration, and Standard. Debbie has had Shameless, and The Walking Wounded indepth women's bible studies, published by New Hope Publishers and Cross Books. Debbie has also published Gilead Now by Westbow Press

Debbie seeks to minister to hurting women who have gone through many trials and tribulations. Debbie, a survivor of abuse, has fought many personal battles, including an eating disorder, and is an active member of AA. Debbie's passion can be seen in the example of Jesus commanding others to take off Lazarus' grave clothes, as she ministers to those trying to become free from past issues as well as personal mistakes.

Debbie currently teaches and writes full time. Debbie is currently training for her second marathon. Debbie was a nationally ranked tennis player who won several state championships, was the eighth ranked amateur in the nation in 1989 in singles and was the 3rd ranked doubles amateur in the nation in 1989. She has coached numerous state champions and has coached on the high school and college level. Debbie enjoys running, reading and spending time with her family. She resides in Little Rock, Arkansas.

TO ORDER DEBBIE'S BOOKS GO TO AMAZON.COM

To contact Debbie about speaking at your church
go to debbievanderslice@yahoo.com

Overview

And the House Was Filled is a ten chapter non-fiction book that takes a parallel look at Mary of Bethany and compares it to a modern day Mary who gave her life for Christ.

Imagine if you will, that you are in the best shape of your life, having just completed your first ever marathon while just weeks pregnant with your second child. Now imagine running, unknowingly, that race with a malignant tumor the size of a small melon in your chest. After hearing the devastating news that you have lymphoma cancer you are encouraged by the doctors to abort your pregnancy and begin immediate chemotherapy. But what if God had something altogether different. What if you did not abort your baby and endured six grueling months of chemotherapy. Imagine this and you have just described a modern day Mary of Bethany.

The author uses this book to instill in readers the incredible sacrifice that one mother made on behalf of her love for Christ and her child, while comparing it to the sacrifice that Mary of Bethany made. Both of these women of God gave the most intimate sacrifice they could when faced with insurmountable odds. What did these two women give in the name of radical sacrifice? Simply put, they gave themselves to The Creator and Giver of Life.

Readers today are no different than the two women in this book. Readers of all ages are encouraged and challenged to live a life of sacrifice before The Lord God Almighty

Chapter Synopses

Chapter 1 Giving from the Heart

This opening chapter brings into focus Martha, prayer partner of the author, and Mary of Bethany and highlights from 1 Samuel 16:7a how God looks at the heart and not the outward appearance of His children. By taking the readers to the Garden of Eden and where sacrifice first manifested itself, readers will be introduced to both women and bring home the fact that each gave sacrifices close to their hearts.

Chapter 2 Giving Completely

By using the scripture, 1 John 4:12, the author keys in on how God desires that we give to Him completely. While many of us may think we have nothing to offer God in terms of sacrifice, the author will encourage readers to make due with what they have. By comparing Mary and the author's friend, Martha, readers will see that each of us do indeed have much to present to God as it relates to the gift of sacrifice.

Chapter 3 Giving Desperately

By using the Psalm 142:6 of David, readers will see how both women were in desperate need of The Father. Mary, who in desperation to show her emotions to Christ before He was to go to the cross, gave Him her most prized possession, a bottle of pure nard, while the author's friend gave Him her health. Both women were in despair to somehow communicate to God her desire for their lives.

Chapter 4 Giving Unselfishly

This chapter talks about the unselfish acts that both women in this book did on behalf of their love for Christ and the life He gave them. Both women paid a high price for their Savior and did not consider what the world thought about their unselfish acts.

Chapter 5 Giving Extraordinarily

This chapter zeroes in on the rare gifts each women gave to Christ while on earth. One woman was always at His feet, while the other used her feet to run the race of life for Him. While the world may tell us that we possess no unusual gifts for God, scripture tells us differently.

Chapter 6 Receiving Blessings

This chapter points out the outcome or results from sacrificing for God. One woman, Mary, received the gift of being remembered in scripture by Christ, while the other woman, Martha, received the gift of a perfectly healthy baby daughter. No matter our circumstances, God blesses the gift of sacrifice.

Chapter 7 Receiving Life

This chapter refers to the unmistakable fact that as believers we not only receive eternal life, but also the abundant life when putting Christ and His Word first. By looking at both women in this book, readers will experience the life altering truth that we can experience an overflowing life of abundance when we sacrifice for God.

Chapter 8 Receiving Grace

Whenever God's children sacrifice great gifts to Him, He provides enough grace sufficient to finish the task. By viewing both women in this book, readers will be comforted that each of us is capable of making it through extremely difficult circumstances via grace from The Father.

Chapter 9 Receiving Peace

This chapter is devoted to the unsurpassing peace that comes from sacrifice. Both women experienced peace beyond measure after very public acts of obedience out of love for their Maker.

Chapter 10 Receiving the Fullness of Christ

This book ends by taking a look at the fullness each of us can have when we enter into a sacrificial relationship with Christ. While each of us gives in different ways to God, each gift is radical when given out of love and devotion to God. Readers will come away having seen a modern day Mary, the author's friend, as well as having walked with Mary of Bethany and her radical sacrifice as well.

Chapter 1

Giving From the Heart

1 Samuel 16:7b "The Lord does not look at the things man looks at. Man looks at the outward appearance, but God looks at the heart." (ESV)

I took a slow, deep breath and tried my best to suck in the tension filled, cold atmosphere of the intensive care room. Only weeks before I had visited my close friend and prayer partner, Martha, in her regular, warm, and jubilant hospital room just moments after she had delivered her second child. Martha, only thirty years old, was now vacillating between life and death right before my eyes, and I was scared of losing her.

Just months before, Martha had run her first ever dreamed about marathon while knowingly pregnant with her second child. However, Martha had run the race unknowingly while harboring a malignant tumor the size of a small melon located in her chest. While Martha had completed the arduous 26.2 mile race, another race would begin for her and all those who loved her. The race of life.

The doctors gave Martha an ultimatum. Abort the baby and begin chemotherapy that very day, or begin a chemotherapy regiment, also that very day, that would more than likely result in deforming the precious life inside her As I entered the ICU room with Martha's husband close behind, I was terrified of messing up the myriad of tubes cohesively keeping Martha alive. Her kidneys were failing and she was in a life-threatening coma. As I approached my dear friend, I heard God's serene and compassionate whisper in my ear. "This is what an heir is. You are entering the holy of holies. It is because of your relationship with Martha that you are being allowed into this intimate place.

I sang a couple of songs to Martha, being ever aware that I was in such a precarious and intimate setting. I talked to Martha, urging her to keep fighting for what we all willed for her. Life.

There were several moments of silence where I looked at this woman of God who had just been through six straight months of chemotherapy before delivering a 100% healthy baby daughter. Surely this child was born of this mother's love.

As I drove home that day, I couldn't help to ponder about those silent moments with Martha. It reminded me of another hushed atmosphere with a woman who loved out of her heart as Martha had. Mary of Bethany.

Mary of Bethany can be found in Mark and John anointing Jesus before He traveled to the cross that fateful Friday. Mary, like my friend Martha, gave out of her heart. In its' purest form it is called sacrifice. But just exactly what is this thing called sacrifice?

According to Webster, sacrifice is defined as "an act of offering to deity something precious; a yielding of something for the sake of something else." In both instances, Mary of Bethany and my friend Martha fulfilled in the purest form of what a sacrifice is.

Where exactly does sacrifice originate? Where can we trace its beginning?

The issue of sacrifice goes all the way back to the Garden of Eden. After Adam and Eve had sinned we see the very first sacrifice. The Garden was merely a glimpse to the finality of The Cross. We see in Genesis 3:21 that God made 'coverings' for Adam and Eve. "The Lord god made garments of skin for Adam and his wife and clothed them." In order for there to be skin coverings, God had to first sacrifice an offering, or animal, for the atonement of Adam and Eve's sin. Hebrews 9:22 says, "In fact, the law requires that nearly everything be cleansed with blood, and without the shedding of blood there is no forgiveness." Thus, there was a yielding of something, in this case, an animal, for the sake of something else, sin. Is this not the foreshadowing of what is to come?

In the Garden that day, God sacrificed an animal out of love for Adam and Eve. He could have just left propitiation, or the substitution for sin, alone. Yet, He didn't. He acts on behalf of Adam and Eve to show them His heart. It is a heart borne out of yielding something for something else.

It is also worth noting that Eve also sacrificed something when she sinned. She sacrificed perfection for sin. Sin never lies dormant in a sea of inactivity. Sin creeps and crawls and eventually walks and talks until we are in the throngs of the consequences of sin. Eve gave up life as she knew it, perfection, for a tainted taste of sin, or imperfection.

Eve, in her blissful environment, traded a sinless, perfected state, with one of sin and shame. Thus, she yielded or sacrificed who she was for a curse. Galatians 3:12 says, "Christ redeemed us from the curse of the law by becoming a curse for us." All of us, whether we realize it or not, sacrifice constantly either to God or to Satan. We either are "with God or against Him." (Luke 11:23)

Just like Eve sacrificed life in paradise for a momentary pleasure, we too fall into the traps of life after trading what is pure and right for what is blemished and wrong. However, like Mary and my friend Martha, we can offer up to God the longings of love in our hearts in order to glorify God.

Isaiah 53:7 describes Christ, The Lamb of God, led like a "lamb to the slaughter." God Incarnate, The Word made flesh, acts as the ultimate sacrifice for us. Thus, the beginning of sacrifice was ordained by God who loved us in our sin to become sin for us. It is in the Garden of Eden then that God requires a sacrifice for His love of obsession; us. Let's take a look at another individual who sacrificed out of love.

By contrast, to Eve's sacrifice, Mary of Bethany is portrayed in the Gospel of Mark and John as anointing Jesus for His burial. Mary, out of love, sacrifices, or yields something expensive, a bottle of pure nard, for the sake of something else. devotion, or love. What exactly did she sacrifice? An expensive perfume. What did she get in return? Love. Out of a heart of love comes the blessing of giving.

Mary of Bethany is always recorded in scripture in the physical position of sitting at Jesus' feet. Thus, we see a humble heart subjecting herself to listening and learning Jesus' ways and teachings. She wants to be physically near Him and listen to Him. While her sister, Martha, cooked and grumbled about Mary doing 'nothing,' Jesus smiled at Mary's heart. Once again, God looks at the heart and not the outer appearance of man. (1 Samuel 16:7b)

Mary interrupts a party and stuns the attendees. According to Jewish law, Mary could have been put to death. However, look at her heart. She humbly enters the party and anoints Jesus' head with perfume and dries his feet with her hair. It was so taboo for women to enter a dinner party that the crowd was stunned. Shocked. In disarray. It is interesting that Mary is not recorded in scripture as being at Christ's crucifixion. Although this doesn't mean she wasn't there, it stands to reason that she would have been mentioned if she were present, as were the other women who were close to Christ. I have often wondered if it was because of her love for Christ that made her stay away. What do you think?

I can think of no other more powerful emotion than love. After all, love beckoned God Himself to endure the shame and death of the cross. The Creator nailed to His own creation. Love normal? Not that day. No more normal than for a holy God who chose to enter the human race and sacrificed His life and love for us, His creation.

Both women took a life altering risk. Perhaps people were shocked when Mary entered the dinner party. More than likely, Martha stunned the doctors by not aborting and enduring six straight months of chemotherapy while pregnant. Martha told me it would be easy and justifiable to have the abortion according to the world's perspective. However, Martha said that it was no accident she was pregnant and had cancer. Martha said it was a heavenly perspective she followed after and that gave her sustaining strength to not abort the life inside her. She said she'd rather obey God and die than to disobey God and live.

I believe Mary and Martha were tender hearted believers that had decided life was worth the risk. Both probably questioned the mundane in life. I truly believe they decided to go for it; to all out encounter and abandon themselves to God. This reminds me of another story about breaking out of the familiar day after day. Sometimes doing the unexpected causes others to question the familiar. Both Mary and Martha defied all odds and decided to experience the spectacular just like Old Red in the following story did. All three had one thing in common; they risked the mundane for the unusual.

> Just like Eve sacrificed life in paradise for a momentary pleasure, we too fall into the abyss of life after trading what is pure and right for what is blemished and wrong. However, like Mary and my friend Martha, we can offer up to God the longings of love in our hearts in order to glorify God. "...and live a life of love, just as Christ loved us and gave himself up for us as a fragrant offering and sacrifice to God." (Ephesians 5:2 ESV)

Chapter 2

Giving Completely

1 John 4:12b "...God lives in us and his love is made complete in us."(ESV)

I entered the hospital room quietly, not wanting to disturb Martha's sleep. Weeks earlier she had miraculously emerged from her life-threatening coma. The prognosis was not good. The lymphoma cancer had spread to her kidneys and over seventy percent of both kidneys were now cancerous. The next twenty four hours I spent with Martha were life altering for one person. Me.

Because Martha was now diagnosed as terminal, preparations were being made with the hospice organization in her hometown. I sat numb from this information and wondered how Martha was taking the news. She had awakened from her nap and was furiously on the phone, calling all dear friends and family and urging them to live on as her legacy. "I'm going away for a while, but we'll be together one day soon," she told a close childhood friend. Martha gave me a thumbs up and appeared to be driven as she talked from person to person and informed them that "we are all terminal." I almost broke down as she reminded her friends and family that "to live is Christ and to die is gain." (Philippians 1:21)

After Martha hung up the phone, she beckoned me to help

clean and fix up her room for visitors. As we tidied up the room, it hit me to the core of my being that God was doing the exact same thing in heaven. John 14:2 says, "In my Father's house are many rooms; if it were not so, I would have told you. I am going there to prepare a place for you." Look at the next couple of verse that tells us that God prepares a place for us. Exodus 23:20 "...and bring you to the place I have prepared." 1 Corinthians 2:9 "No eye has seen, no ear has heard, no mind has conceived what God has prepared for those who love him." I cleaned up the hospital room for Martha with tears in my eyes. "Deb, what do you think of making the room a little more like home? What about making it more personal?" Yes. God was at work on Martha's place in heaven. Preparations were being made. Eternal preparations.

Just as Martha prepared her hospital room for visitors, so too Mary of Bethany made preparations for Christ. Look at Mark 14:3-9 "While in Bethany, reclining at the table in the home of a man known as Simon the Leper, a woman came with an alabaster jar of very expensive perfume, made of pure nard. She broke the jar and poured the perfume on his head. Some of those present were saying indignantly to one another, 'Why this waste of perfume? It could have been sold for more than a year's wages and the money given to the poor.' And they rebuked her harshly. 'Leave her alone,' said Jesus. 'Why are you bothering her? She has done a beautiful thing to me. The poor you will always have with you, and you can help them any time you want. But you will not always have me. She did what she could. She poured perfume on my body beforehand to *prepare* for my burial. I tell you the truth, wherever the gospel is preached throughout the world, what she has done will also be told, in memory of her.'"

The Greek word here for prepare means to make ready. Mary is preparing and getting Christ ready for His suffering and death. Jesus knew He was going to the cross in the next several days, and I believe Mary knew He was about to suffer a horrible death and injustice. Thus, she risked her life by entering Simon the Leper's home and anointing Jesus with the perfume.

When we prepare our hearts and give ourselves completely to Him as an undying sacrifice, God prepares us physically, emotionally, and spiritually to go the distance until we see Him face to face in our personally prepared home, heaven.

Just like my friend Martha, Mary gave herself completely to Christ before He was about to die. Martha offered up her body as "a living sacrifice to God" (Romans 12:1, ESV)

Just as Christ did. Mary, Martha, and Jesus sacrificed life and death *completely* in order that God would be glorified. Look at 1 John 2:5 "But if anyone obeys his word, God's love is truly made complete in him."

Out of true love comes complete obedience. The Greek word here for complete means to make full or accomplish. I believe scripture tells us a clue to the byproduct of giving completely to God. Look at the following verses and make note of the word that seems to go hand and hand with complete. John 15:11 "I have told you this so that your joy may be complete." Philippians 2:2 "...then make my joy complete." 1 John 1:3-4 "And our fellowship is with the Father and with his Son, Jesus Christ. We write this to make our joy complete." 2 John 12b says, "Instead, I hope to visit you and talk with you face to face, so that our joy may be complete."(ESV)

All four verses indicate that with the complete or full giving of ourselves to God, joy follows. It may be difficult to understand, but joy is different from happy. Happy is an emotional feeling; joy is a deep, abiding spiritual gift. Galatians 5:2 says, "But the fruit of the Spirit is love, joy..."

It is important to note that both Mary and Martha sacrificed completely what they *had*, not what they didn't have . Mark 14:7-8 says, "The poor you will always have with you and you can help them any time you want. But you will not always have me. *She did what she could.*" Sometimes I think we give half-heartedly because we think of all the things we don't have, such as money. We think to ourselves, "my sacrifice is so small it won't matter." You see friend God delights in us giving or sacrificing completely what we can, not what we cannot. Sure, we may not have a lot of money, but there are other ways to offer up to God a sacrifice and give from the heart.

Mary sacrificed her most prized possession, a bottle of pure nard. Martha gave her body up for God to do with as He saw fit. How do we sacrifice completely? That's easy. Any sacrifice given from the heart and out of an obedient love and devotion is a beautiful sacrifice. "Ephesians 5:2ESV "And like a life of love, just as Christ loved us and gave himself up for us as a fragrant offering and sacrifice to God…"

There are several different biblical types of sacrifices. Let's take a look at each of them and then highlight the type of sacrifice Mary and Martha made to God. First of all, the Old Testament defines sacrifice as "the religious act belonging to worship in which offering is made to God of some material object being consumed in the ceremony, in order to attain, restore, maintain, or celebrate friendly relations with the deity." (The New International Dictionary of the Bible, P.56)

The motives of sacrifice of course, vary with each individual. There is the sin sacrifice, which we first see in the Garden of Eden with Eve, and end with Christ at the cross. Sin offerings before Christ were made for the whole congregation on the Day of Atonement. On that day, an unblemished animal would be offered up to God for the sins of the people as a community. Is it no wonder then that Christ, our high priest, offered Himself up to God as a sin offering for the sins of *all* mankind. A sacrifice given by One Man stood firm for the sake of all people who would believe in Him.

Next there was the guilt sacrifice and was a "special kind of sin offering and was sacrificed for transgressions where restitution or other legal satisfaction was made." (The NIV Dictionary of the Bible (p.76)

The burnt sacrifice was for the purpose of propitiation as well as the whole consecration of the person to God. The burnt sacrifice was a continual sacrifice because it went on throughout the Jewish generations. Look at Exodus 29:42 (ESV) "For the generations to come this burnt offering is to be made regularly at the entrance to the Tent of Meeting before the Lord." This sacrifice was offered up twice daily.

The fellowship sacrifice was an offering of gratitude to God as well as fellowship with Him. Two kinds of fellowship sacrifice were the praise and freewill offerings. These sacrifices could be lifted up in either rejoicing times, or else very solemn times.

A drink sacrifice was made to accompany all burnt offerings and all fellowship offerings. "They did not accompany sin and guilt offerings." (The NIV Dictionary of the Bible p. 87) This particular sacrifice, the drink offering, was wine that was poured out on the altar.

Other sacrifices were the vegetable or bloodless sacrifice, as well as the grain sacrifice. The grain sacrifices, in particular, accompanied the other sacrifices in the morning and evening burnt offerings.

What kind of sacrifice did Mary and Martha make? Both gave of themselves and therefore were fellowship offerings, particularly the freewill sacrifice, or the giving of themselves. In addition to offering a freewill sacrifice, Mary and Martha's lives were then poured out as drink offerings. Look at what Philippians 2:17 (ESV) says. "But even if I am being poured out like a drink offering on the sacrifice and service coming form your faith, I am glad and rejoice with all of you."(ESV)-

Out of the giving completely of themselves came true blessings in the form of sacrifices. Mary gave what she could. Her perfume was a sweet aroma to Christ. "For we are to God the aroma of Christ...the fragrance of life." (2 Corinthians 2:15a, 16b ESV)

Martha, who also gave of herself, offered up freely to God her body; a freewill offering. "...a fragrant offering, an acceptable sacrifice, pleasing to God." (Philippians 4:18, ESV))

Never once did I hear Martha complain of her draw or lot in life. No tears, no anger, no lamenting her fate. This caused two things to happen in my life. One I was truly blessed to have been her friend and prayer partner. Because I spent a lot of time on the tennis courts, I didn't have much time to develop friendships. Thus, when I met Martha at the age of 27, I began to experience friendship on a deep level. Two, Martha taught me that the road God chose for me is a different road He may chose for someone else. Out of these two facets of Christian living she taught me, the following writings occurred. In conclusion, what is your road? How can we, as fallen humans, sacrifice freely to God? I believe all it takes is an obedient heart full of love for The Master. Remember, He provides what we have to offer Him. Let's start giving completely to Him today.

What God starts He will finish. Look at" Jn. 19:20b." It is fiished. God saves us completely. We are sealed with God's redemption and have life in heaven. God loves us too much to let us flounder about like a fish.

Does every believer grow? No. Does my belief change my life. Yes and no. Yes, we are saved but not grow is one way to go. Why not? Maybe it is an addiction. Alcoholism, Bulima and Anorexia. We are given the power to change we have to give Him completely everything. Everything. It is an ongoing process called sanctification. It doesn't end until we see Christ face to face.

God does not half way do things. He is either all in or all out. He is never lukewarm, like us. Call if what you will. I know it sounds unlike God but remember He is patient. When we give yp something for God, it is a sweet aroma to God like Martha's sacrifice of her body. Others live because of her death. She completely gave her body to Christ.

> `We do not deserce Christ. H e gave His life completely to us. Would you die for a lie? Of course not. Christ was The Turth, The spotless lamb of God. We serve death, not life. He gave to us completely.

> 1 Thess 5:23 "now may the God of peace Himself savituy you completely..."(ESV)

Job 23:14 "For He will complete what he appoints for me and many such things are in his mind." (ESV)

Philippians 1:6 "And I am sure of ths, that he who begain a good work in you will bring it to eompletion at the day of Jesus Cheist." (ESV)

Which verse spoke to you. None or all? I have fallen down in my walk about a million times, in thought, word, and deed. When I confess it to God it is like water on a parched throat.

When we confess we are giving completely our lives to Christ. To think we have nothing to confess if an arrogant and bogus attitude. Let our confession be every before us each and every day. Let us go before God and tell or talk to Him for just five minutes a day. Then 10 minutes the next day and so and behold it will be for longer each and every time. God walked and talked with the outcasts who didn't know the four spiritual laws. All we must do is bring Him our honesty. That's it. No long drawn out prayer. All we have to do is bring ourselves to Him. He does or did the rest. He completely restores us. It is all about Him, not our sin. He completely saves us and restores us. It is all about Him. Our part? We simply sin. He will grow us on His timetable. Not ours or society. On His terms and His time table. Is that a benevelent God or what?!

Chapter 3

Giving Desperately

Psalm 142:6a "Listen to my cry, for I am in desperate need."

I raced to the sno cone stand two blocks from the hospital at neck breaking speed. I reasoned that if I were to hit anyone I could carry them to the emergency room nearby. My thoughts were frantic as I pulled up in my minivan and shouted in a desperate voice to the teeny bopper who ran the small seasonal sno cone stand.

"I need a twenty-five dollar gift certificate immediately," I said to him, almost hyperventilating.

The sixteen year-old looking boy glanced at me. His wide eyes and blank stare gave me reason to restate my request. So I did.

He looked at me again like I was out of my mind. "I'm sorry but I don't think we do gift certificates here."

I thrust my twenty-five dollars up on the tiny counter laced with purple and red stains and said, "Well, here's the money, and you better get me a gift certificate fast. Just write me a note or something please. I'm in a hurry."

Still looking at me like I had just come from another planet devoid of life, the teenager replied, "Well, I'll call my manager but we really don't do that kind of thing because no one has ever done it.

I felt like yelling at this boy who had no facial hair that I had never watched a close friend dying before in a hospital who was requesting lime sno cones. I felt like screaming to this youngster, "Well, I don't do death either buddy boy," but somehow managed to find some other choice words for him.

I told the sno cone worker that I would return in thirty minutes to collect my gift certificate. Never had I been so bold before. But never had death been so near.

My close friend and prayer partner of two years lay less than two blocks away in ICU. Martha had recently come out of a life threatening coma and the respirator tube had been removed. A doctor asked Martha if she wanted anything. Martha said yes. A lime sno cone.

It was understood by all who visited Martha in ICU that she was not expected to live much longer. We were allowed to visit often, unlike many other ICU patients who could only have visitors every two hours. I wish I could tell you the doctor didn't have tears in his eyes but he did. When Martha finally had the tubes removed from her throat and the strength to talk again, this man of medicine leaned over and asked Martha to name whatever she wanted most of all with food and drink. I'll never forget the sparkle in her eyes and surprise on her face when she said, "you mean anything at all?" So, on a hot summer day in late July that year, a lime sno cone was beckoned. As I left the ICU room that day and got into the elevator, I lost all composure and drove at neck breaking speed to the little sno cone stand two blocks down the road.

You see, a long time ago a woman named Mary of Bethany did an insane thing too. Instead of going to a sno cone stand and ordering a twenty-five dollar gift certificate, Mary instead went and poured a bottle of nard, an expensive perfume, on Jesus' head and then dried his feet with her hair. Why? Because Mary loved Jesus. Because Mary was *desperate* to somehow communicate the deep love within her for her friend before He was to die.

Let's look at Mary again. Notice what Jesus' disciples do that day a woman comes barging in with tears into their nice dinner party. They ridicule her. They tell Jesus she wasted the perfume on Him when it could have been sold and the money given to the poor. That was the tangible world's response. But watch heaven's intangible response from God Almighty. Watch God at work here when the world scoffs at a heart language that only the poor in spirit can speak. Jesus said Mary had done a beautiful thing. Then He goes on to say that she would be remembered forever for what she had done. Does God know our pain? Does He remember things we have given up for His sake? Oh yes, without a doubt. It's a language Jesus knows all too well. For it is a language born out of love.

Before you go thinking I am comparing myself to Mary of Bethany, let me assure you I am not doing so. I doubt very seriously Mary ever called a sno cone worker a slow poke as she ordered a certificate. Did I mention I got frustrated at the sno cone worker that day? Funny how details get lost sometimes.

I don't agree with the scholars when they say Mary of Bethany anointed Jesus for the purpose to prepare Him for His death. Yes, that much is true, for scripture tells us that. But Mary's anointing via the perfume was merely a byproduct of her devotion to Him. Jesus was Mary's ticket to who she was. What she was. Mary pouring the pure nard on Jesus that day and drying His feet with her hair were desperate acts of love.

Notice what Mary and my friend Martha had in common. Sacrificial love. Mary took something very expensive and dear to her heart, same with Martha, and thrust it upon God out of love. Notice once again the response of heaven as the world scoffed. Jesus Himself said Mary would be remembered for this act. Jesus called her gift beautiful.

Stunning isn't it? God tells this woman of no status in the world's eyes that she will be remembered for her beautiful sacrifice. Why? Because the key was Mary's heart. That is the ticket God is after in us humans. After all, didn't God's own heart draw Him to the cross out of love? And only the heart can love. What is God's response to Martha not aborting and going through months and months of chemotherapy with no assurance that things would work out? Oh, if heaven's walls could talk, and they do, I think we'd hear Jesus saying the same to Martha. What a beautiful gift of sacrificial love.

Notice a dramatic detail about Mary of Bethany. Mary risks it all and enters the home of Simon the Leper. Mary goes alone. She is desperate to somehow show her friend how much she loves Him and wants to comfort Him in His dying days. True love will stand alone if necessary. Why? Because the tug of the heart is the most powerful force in the universe. How do I know that? Why else did Christ, God Almighty, go to the cross?

Let's now take a look at what the word desperate means. Desperate is defined as "being beyond or almost beyond hope." (Webster's Dictionary) Mary and Martha had one thing in common-they were both almost beyond the hope of conveying to God how much they loved Him. When faced with life or death situations, they chose the way of diffidence.

Out of despair and almost out of hope, both women sacrificed certainty for uncertainty. They gave everything, the objects that were most important to them and thrust them upon God. Out of great desperation came great gifts of love.

Mary of Bethany uttered no words as she anointed Christ that day at Simon the Leper's home. Jesus had been at Mary, Martha, and Lazarus' home just days prior to this dinner party at Simon's house. A pivotal question might be why didn't Mary anoint Jesus when He was at their home? Why did she wait?

I believe Mary was a deep thinker. For example, we see her listening at Jesus' feet every time she is in scripture. Perhaps she was pondering what Jesus said and taught. More than likely, Mary took to heart Jesus' words. I believe Mary thought and thought about what Jesus said to those closest to Him when He said, "...the Son of Man will be handed over to be crucified." (Matthew 26:21b)

I believe Mary waited and waited and thought and thought of

what she could do to communicate her love to Jesus before He was to face His final days. Maybe Mary couldn't think of anything to give Him. She was without a gift.

Finally, in desperation, she grabs her most beloved and richest possession-her bottle of pure nard. Its' worth was one full year of wages. It was her ace in the hole. Her college tuition. She takes her gift and runs, as if for her life, to where her Savior is. Her mentor. Her Lord and God. Once there, she bursts into the house and interrupts the conversation. The only sound in the room was Mary's heavy breathing as she tries her best to pull herself together. It's no use. She breaks the bottle with all her force, sobs uncontrollably and wails in deep desperation. She is, at best, a desperate woman, sacrificing her most intimate possession for The One who is The Ultimate Possession.

While Mary sacrificed her most precious possession, my friend Martha also gave up all she knew to give; her body. After Martha had been terminally diagnosed, she sought out alternative healing treatments. "Deb, make me a shark cartridge cocktail, would you. And don't forget to make me a cranberry chaser to force it down with." Martha was desperately trying to cling to life, even after being diagnosed as terminal. She had, in all good faith, given up her body as a "living sacrifice" for Christ. (Romans 12:1, ESV)

In Martha's dying days, she created the most spectacular artwork. Martha, an artist, painted a mural for her children in their bedrooms, as well as other inspiring works. Martha desperately was trying to communicate her love for her children through the most intimate thing she could physically do-her artwork.

Martha, in a loss for words, communicated through her artwork her love for not only her children, but also for her Lord. On one particular night in the hospital, around 10pm., Martha asked me to read the Psalms to her as she drifted in and out of sleep with the morphine drip connected to her fragile hand. As I read to my prayer partner, it became apparent that Martha was desperately trying to listen to the Word, even as she was so ill.

Desperation can either draw us closer to God, or make us flee like cowards. Both Mary of Bethany and Martha were desperate to show their love and lives to God. Remember the next time you face insurmountable odds that God loves us in our desperation. We can all sacrifice from the heart. All it takes is to reveal to God how much He means to us. May we all become desperate in our weak and feeble attempts to honor God. He specializes in desperate acts of love.

Chapter 4

Giving Unselfishly

1 Corinthians 13:3

"if ...I give away all that I have,...but do not love I gain nothing." (ESV)

I never ever could explain the life and death of my first prayer partner. As I said earlier I went to an evangelism explosion class in my Dallas church to more effectively learn how to share the gospel. Not knocking on doors but rather in my relationships. To learn how to share Christ. I was sitting in this class and was doubting my own salvation experience. I t was a crisis. What to do now? I picked out the most confident female there and asked her what the unpardonable sin was. Not for me mind you but for a friend. Martha as I would later learn said, "Oh that is rejecting Christ and his sacrifice for you." Whew, I was safe. Then I gathered my confidence and asked this girl named Martha if she would be my prayer partner. She said yes. Two home runs in one day. I was rocking.

Martha and I became best buddies very quickly. On many occasions I found a homemade loaf of bread on my doorstep. From Martha of course. We were both gift givers and spent much time praying for each other and people on our prayer lists. Martha went on to have a boy and a few months later I had a girl. We got involved with a trade out and I kept her son a full day and she kept my daughter a full day. No need for daycare. We came to share with each other the good, bad, and ugly in our lives.

For the life of me I cannot grasp why Martha had to get cancer. Why her? She had so much ahead of her. Why now God. Why not 10 or 20 years later?

It is a question that God has not revealed to me. I did however get a glimpse of her about a year or two ago. I had a major stroke and I remember being in the ambulance and being on top of the paramedics who said, there is no pulse. I was "dead" for two minutes. It was during this two minutes that I was in a lush field with Martha in a shin length robe and was walking hand in hand with a man with a beard and should length hair, auburn, and had a beard. Martha ran to me and I said, "Martha you've got hair" and she said, "But of course." She was leaving and giggling like a school girl. I told her I wanted to go with them too. She said, "It's not your time yet." It remains my most vivid dreams/visions ever. I do not remember them doing cpr on me. That whole experience is gone. But I do remember when I was dead for two minutes and seeing Martha again. It was one of the most loving things I have ever experienced in my life. Is there a God? Oh yes. Is He alive. Oh yes. Do I fear death. Not any more I don't. Would you?

One of my favorite songs is by Twila Paris. She perfectly describes how beautiful it is when Christ sacrificed His life for us. When we give all we can it is a beautiful sacrifice to the Lord. He knows our heart and it is stunning to Him. He knows our pain. Our hopes. Our desires. Our shortcomings. And yet God still uses us. When He looks at us He sees our hearts that are filled with Christ. Is there nothing more pleasing to Him than a sacrifice to honor Him. I think it is His favorite thing. To take a broken and bruised life and turn it into something so beautiful. He is in the business of that. Look at Twila Paris' song below. It still blows me away. Even after discovering it over a decade ago.

When my friend Martha had the size of a tumor the size of a small melon in her chest she had to make a choice. She was only about 4 or 5 weeks along in her pregnancy. The doctors gave her an ultimatum. Abort and do chemotherapy that day or keep the baby and still do chemotherapy that very day. Martha told me it was an easy choice. She would do chemo baby and all. The experts said the baby would not survive the intense chemo or the baby would not be healthy when the baby was born.

We still went on our power walks, ate homemade bread, and went to our favorite place...Cracker Barrel. I prayed like I never have prayed before. For both the baby and Martha to be 100% healthy. It was a long pregnancy. As soon as Madison was born, 100% healthy at 4.0lbs, I fell on my knees and thanked God for a healthy baby.

As soon as the baby was born, later on that night, Martha resumed her chemotherapy. It was a couple of days before I got the bad news. The lymphoma had spread everywhere. 70% over her entire body. I fell to the floor.

"Please don't take her take me. She is so much a better believer than I am. She can further your kingdom more than I sure can. She is light years ahead in her relationship than I am with you. Please God."

Not sure what to do I sped over to the hospital at once. I knocked and went in. She was feeding Madison a bottle. She explained how the doctors said her milk would not come in due to her illness. Martha's phone rang constantly. Congrats and well wishers, and family members flooded her phone line.

I heard her say to one close friend, "I have to go away for a while but we'll be together soon." That was just like Martha. Always thinking positively. I turned my back and went to the bathroom nearby. Wasn't that just like her. Finding the positive when faced with a terminal illness. The glass was always half full for her and I always saw it as half empty. Maybe that is why we were such good friends and prayer partners.

During Martha's final weeks at home I saw her on a ladder

in Madison's room painting an incredible mural. She made me promise to accept and love her husband's new wife once he remarried. So I promised her. The she took my hand and said it was going to be ok. She would soon be whole and happy and healed. Heaven bound. Paradise. Eternal life. I said I would and that I swore to her that I would tell her children over and over how much they were loved by their momma. As I drove away that day I told God He had better have one hell of a place for her in heaven. That is what I said to God that day. I was not pleased with Him at all. Not at all.

Martha passed away on a cold November night. In fact, it snowed lightly that night. I felt as though God were saying, " She lived a pure life just like the snow tonight. Don't you see my hand in this, Deb?" I was overwhelmed at Martha's life. She accepted me with all my flaws. She knew all about me and still hung around. That was so out of control. I felt my life was now spinning out of control. Then God nudged me and said, "I am still in control. I am still on the throne. I called Martha home because it was her time. I've got her now and I had her the whole time she was sick

Mary of Bethany and my buddy Martha gave of themselves. What could Mary of Bethany give to Christ. He was about to go to the cross. What on earth could she give him? She had no real money. No one in the family had real tangible money. But wait, Mary had a pure jar of nard, an expensive perfume. It was worth a year's wages. It was all that the family had. Mary listened to Christ and was by His side every time we see her in scripture. But Martha was busy with housekeeping and concerned mainly not with Jesus, but whether or not the house was tidy or not.

But Mary had the ticket. She was always at Jesus' feet in the Gospels. That takes true humility. She broke the jar of perfume to prepare Christ for His burial. She had a tender heart. Martha was more concerned as to whether or not the house was clean or not.

"Six days before the Passover, Jesus therefore came to Bethany were Lazarus was and his two sisters, Mary and Martha. Remember Lazarus, whom Jesus had raised from the dead. So they gave a dinner for Him there. Martha served, and Lazarus was one of those reclining with Him at the table. Mary therefore took a pound of expensive perfume made form pure nard, and anointed the feet of Jesus and wiped his feet with her hair. The house was filled with the fragrance of perfume.(John 12:1-3, ESV)

Mary did not have any money. Only the pure nard, or perfume. She gave to Christ out of her heart. The perfume was the money maker. But that is all she had. I think she knew Jesus was on his way to the cross. She wanted Him to smell good because she knew He was about to be killed. She gave of herself. She thrust upon him the only thing she valued the most. His friendship was well worth it.

Does this sound familiar to you?. A young woman who loved Christ gave her body, more or less, to God and offered up her pregnancy also to Him. There was no assurance everything would work out. They gave to the Lord. Both gave from their hearts. They gave what they had not what they didn't. And the house was filled with the fragrance of the perfume. That was my prayer partner. My friend.

Whatever you have to give Him, give it over to Him. You may think I mean life and death like my friend. But wait. Anything at all is sufficient. Anything from your heart. Like Ash Wednesday. As long as it is of value to you then give it over to God. I gave up caffeine last year. Yes, had a hard time waking up in the morning but it was a sacrifice nonetheless. And God knew how important it was to me and my waking up schedule.

We do not deserve God's grace. The Bible says while we were sinners Christ died for us. (Romans 5:28 ESV). He was the real deal. The long awaited Messiah. The King of Kings. The Holy One of Israel. The Morning Star. The Star of David. Well, you get the picture.We think about numero uno all the time. How will this affect me. What's in it for me. No, we do not deserve God's unselfishness. His love. His forgiveness. His compassion. His life. He gave up His life so that we might live. Sounds like another story in this book doesn't it? A mother who gave up her life for the sake of her child. True love sacrifices. I see it all the time.

You know I would do pretty good in life if I didn't get in the way of myself. I am my own worst enemy. I can go days without eating and then I will binge eat. Laxatives? Yes. I wish you were reading a book by someone who has it all together. But you don't . I wish you were reading a book by someone who is perfect. But you don't . You have me. You are stuck with me. I take great comfort in the fact that I don't have to tell you I am perfect and full of advice. Instead you have an author who has ventured down some dark corridors. I 've been through the ringer. I have lost those that I have loved and still cry about them at the drop of a hat. But thank God He has gone on ahead of me. He knows what lies ahead. He is my rock. My fortress. I tend to get stuck sometimes. Sometimes I get in the muck and mire of being a victim instead of a survivor. But alas, I will make it through. I am a survivor. You are too.

After Martha died I was so angry at God. Yes, I knew she was in a better place. Yes, I knew that life goes on. However, my world did not go as smoothly as some believers go when they lose a loved one. I had downright rage at God. Why not take an atheist? Or a crime infested person? Why? Why her? Although I will never understand his reason for taking her at the ripe old age of 30, I have come to accept it. While I may never know the reason why, it is not my job to tell God how to run his kingdom. We may never know the reason why God chooses to take some home sooner than others. I am baffled. At a loss. After Martha died I was at a loss with my walk with God. I felt I was living life in slow motion. I also learned that in losing a loved one you must be brave. That or crawl in a hole. I decided right then and there that it was the brave and courageous who go on with their lives. And so would I. Even if it seemed so wrong to me. I feel as though I got plan B. Plan A, the one I wanted was nowhere to be found. I was forced to suck it up and be brave. Plan B. Even if I did not feel like it. Being brave is not being unafraid; it is moving forward in the face of a frightening situation. One brave step at a time

Think about the bravest person that you know. What is it that makes this person so brave? We read about it and see it on tv all the time. It is when a man/woman risks his life for the life of another trapped in a car or burning building. But those are the obvious choices. What about the woman who goes into counseling trying to break the chains of abuse?After Martha died I needed major counseling. But I didn't go right away. I waited a couple of years. I searched for just the right therapist. That took another year. Finally I found the rigtht person. I needed someone understanding about getting stuck in the muck and mire of grief. Someone who wouldn't judge me or cram scripture down my throat. Finally I found the right person. I was severely depressed. I found a doctor also who was patient and kind. Presto I had a support team. And I found the right church who was understanding of me and my struggles. Not a fire and brimstone atmosphere. A graceful and peaceful congregation. Because my support team was with me for the long haul, I think that is key if I want to change and live for Christ. My congregation is the best in the world. They have helped me change into the person I am becoming. A sincere, loving, and patient believer. They teach me how to give unselfishly. They fill up my life with the aroma of Christ. It is all about giving. When we give of ourselves in anyway we can it is a sweet aroma that fills up our home, church, work, or wherever you hang your hat or wherever you are at that exact moment. Sacrifice is not merely in four walls. It can be on a football field, baseball dugout, hospital bed, nursing home, or your own home. Sacrifice is like the engergizer bunny... it keep on going and going and going...well you get the picture.

Chapter 5

Giving Extraordinarily

Ephesians 3:20

"Now to Him who is able to do far more abundantly than we ask or think, according to the power at work within us." (ESV)

Sacrifice. We hear it all the time. We through it around without really thinking it about it. Sure, around Lent we may give up or sacrifice something close to our heart...like ice cream, caffeine, alcohol, or overeating. But what is the real definition of sacrifice? I think my best buddy Martha paid the ultimate sacrifice. She gave her body and cancer over to the Lord. Was it difficult? Oh yes. She did not terminate her pregnancy like the doctor suggested. There was a precious life inside of her. She went through months of chemotherapy and radiation with that precious life inside her. The doctors said the baby would not survive the chemo and radiation. Martha told them, ok. Or would not be healthy. Martha said ok.

Because I was her prayer partner I felt like it was my duty to call every believer I knew and ask them to pray for Martha and the life inside her. Never have I prayed so hard in my life for something. A healthy baby and her mama to be cured.

I spent close to three hours a day in prayer. From 9am-12noon I would walk and pray. I could care less who saw me mumbling to myself. I was after all, Martha's prayer partner.

Martha would tell me over and over after she was terminal to pray for her two precious children and for them to be immersed in the Word. She would tell me to read the Word to them over and over. Now, many years later understand. God word does not come back void. He will answer prayer. Yes, no, or wait. We may not like His answer, but He will respond to our prayer in one form or fashion.

Martha said God 's Word the key. That He is the key to life. Like a sponge, I soaked up what all Martha was telling me. "Deb, don't mourn me for too long. Get on with your life. Have another best friend soon. Learn how to love God deeper and deeper with my death."

She had accepted her lot in life. I had not. We were miles and miles apart in accepting her terminal illness. But I did go to God and His Word after Martha passed away.I needed answers like nobody's business. Martha sensed my frustration at her predicament one night in the hospital. She told me that at any time I was at a loss to turn to God and His Word

When someone gives extraordinarily in our lives we take notice. The fireman who goes in one last time to save the child. The lifeguard who puts his life on the line to dive in to save the child. The good Samatian who helps the lost individual and points him/her in the right direction. All these are commendable acts one can surely see. But what if God had a modern day hero in terms of life for life?

When Martha got the news she was pregnant I was so excited for her. She had just run her first ever dreamed about marathon. But she went to the doctor to see if the marathon had resulted in a pulled stomach muscle. She was only two or three month pregnant. She and her husband were sent to test after test. Then, when this man of medicine told her the devastating news...a tumor the size of a canalope pressing agaist her sternum, she and her husband had a choice to make. abort the fetus and begin chemo that very day or the other alternative...not abort and begin chemo that very day. Not what you would call a win/win situation. Martha was adamant. This precious life inside her was not merely a fetus but a precious life. She would not abort. Bring on chemo. Martha was ready for it. For the fight. For the pregnancy. Her life, after all, was in God's hand. What safer place could she be?

Martha endured chemo and radiation month after month. She had a ton of sonograms. Martha said she prayed and prayed, as did the believers in her chuch, and Martha was at her whits end of what she could do. When they put a port in her chest without any numbing shot or pain medicine, I knew then she was the toughest and most dedicated believer I had ever known. She explained how the medaport was so they could put all her meds in her quickly and was far easier for the nurses to give medicine than stick her writst or arm over and over again.

> Romans 12:1 "Therefore I urge you,brothers nd
> sisters, in view of God's mercy, to offer,your bodies
> as a living sacrifice holy and pleasing to God-this
> is your true and proper worship." (ESV)

I have never seen a body offered up to God as a living sacrifice as my friend Martha gave up. She had no choice but to do chemo and radiation. Without it she and they baby would die. With it she might live and so might the baby. What to do? Talk about a tough assignment. Martha chose chemo. I got on the phone asking all friends and relatives to pray for Martha and the baby. Some people were nice and some think she should have opted for an abortion. That was not even on the table. It was damned if you do and damned if you didn't. Talk about a predicament. Martha said it was an easy choice.She would talk chemo, baby and all.So I got behind her decision and would support her through thick and thin.

It was an easy choice for many of us, after all the baby was still a fetus. Not according to Martha. The fetus inside her was a life. Ordained by God. Set apart since the foundation of the earth. Ordained by the Lord of Lords. This fetus was a breathing human being. No one would have blamed Martha and her husband if they aborted the fetus. No. Simply put she put her foot down. This was a life inside of her. Breathing human being. She would take chemo baby and all. Ok, Martha made her decision. Only Martha could endure 7 months of chemo and radiation and still carry this child to term. She was the toughest gal I knew. And I have known some pretty tough tennis players in my lifetime.

When Martha died I was in shock. I thought God was just grandstanding. Waiting until the last second to swoop in and heal her. Then I thought that we were maybe in the last days and God would beem us up Scotty. No dice. Why take her? Why not somebody that wasn't living for you. Why not a devil worshipper? Why?

And then Martha died. In November. The night she died it snowed. It was the earliest recorded snowfall in Dallas. It was as it God were saying to me, "Deb, she lived a pure life. I've got her. She is safe and sound and healthy and whole with me. Don't worry, I've got her. This next song exemplifies the wonder of heaven. Yes, Martha was safe and sound.

Whenever we see Mary of Bethany she is at the feet of Christ. That shows humility.Why would Mary break open the jar of perfume and pour it on Jesus' feet? It was a spur of the moment thing. It is weren't she would have gotten a towel from the kitchen to dry His feet with. First, at impulse she grabs the only thing of value. The perfume that cost over a year's wages. Why on earth did she do this? I think it was because she knew Jesus was about to go to the cross and die. He friend. Her Savior. Her Redeemer. She knew He was about to be buried and wanted Him to smell good. Funny but true I think. Death has a certain smell to it, doesn't it. He was not going to smell, but be adorned with perfume and spices. I think Mary knew He was about to die. Martha was too busy cleaning the house to notice that kind of situation.

You see God is interested in the detail of our lives. If you are afraid to go to God with a particular prayer request, you are totally wrong. God is the God of details. If you need $4.09 for the gas bill and pray for that over an over, will either say yes to your request, or no, or wait. I love to pray the outlandish or extravagant requests and watch God do His work in and through us.Some believers think God is a coke machine. In goes our requests and out comes our desires. God loves us too much to be a coke machine. If He loves us He will sometimes say no, or not yet.

If I had been God...let me take that in for a moment. If I had been God I would have zapped everyone to hell and made them suffer for sending me to the cross. But God loved us so much that He, God, left the all-you-can-eat-buffet, and endured the human emotions we have and died for us. And He was God!

How do you like them apples. God crucified on the cross. For us. Our sins. Redemption. Salvation. Good thing I wasn't God. I would have stayed in heaven with all the angels circling the throne saying, "Holy Holy Lord God." Yup everyone would have been zapped to hell and I would be eating the no calorie pizza and ice cream. But alas, I am not God. Good thing.

Chapter 6

Receiving Blessings

James 1:17

"Every good gift and every perfect giftt is from above, coming down from the Father of lights with whom there is no variation or shadow due to change." (ESV)

I had a pastor tell me once in Martha's hospital room to "not miss this blessing." I felt like shoving the bed pan up his bottom. Let's see about that. Is that a blessing for him? I think not.

I think or rather depise the believer who says, Praise God," I have hemmoroids. Or praise God we are penniless this month. Or praise God I got fired today. Or praise God, my son was just picked up by police for DWI. I totally believe all things work together for good and are called according to His purpose." (Romans 8:28, ESV). It say all things WORK TOGETHER for good. Not all things are good.

I cannot stand the believer that we see as a victor in every circumstance. They are always quoting this verse. Inappropriately, I might add. If we always praised God for everything, we are a hoax. Our faith is weak. What Deb? If a believer's son is killed by a drunk driver, that is horrible. If someone says don't miss this blessing, then you have my full permission to knock him off his high horse.

We are told to mourn with those who mourn.Ecclesiates tells us there is"a time to laugh; a time to mourn." Eccl. 3:4, ESV) To get stuck in denial is what happened to me after my Martha passed away.

Look up these verses. They are all about receiving blessings. Let these verses immerse you and wrap you in love.

Numbers 6:24-26 "The Lord bless you and keep you; The Lord make his face to shine upon you and give you peace" (ESV)

Romans 15:13 "The Lord lift up his countenance upon you and give you peace May the God of hope fill you with all joy and peace in believing, so that by the power of the Holy Spirit you may abound in hope." (ESV)

Philippians 4:19 "And my God will supply every need of yours according to his riches in glory in Christ Jesus"

James 1:12 "Blessed is the man who remains steadfast under trial, for when he has stood the test he will receive the 'crown of life' which God has promised to those who love him."(ESV)

Which verse out of these is your favorite? My would have to be Philippians 4:19. I clung to this one when Martha was sick. I must have said is 1,000 times during her final days. I was quite a needy person but tried to remain a rock for Martha and her family.

Martha's mom paid me the highest compliment I have ever received. She said of all of Martha's friends I loved her the most. I asked her how she could tell, and she said who goes and gets a 25 dollar gift sno cone certificate for a friend. I said she was my first real best friend because of all my tennis days and not having time for friendships. I told her that God blessed me 10 million times fold with the friendship of Martha. She simply broke the mold.

I never thought I would have any more friends/best friends after Martha died. But lo and behold look what God did. He has blessed me with a church and more friends I can shake a stick at. I even have a favorite friend. Or best friend if Martha were to know the truth. Sometimes out of great sacrice comes great relationships. At least that has been my case. I hope it is your case too.See if you can relate to this song.

Chapter 7

Receiving Life

1Corinthians 7:17a

"Only let each person lead the life that the Lord has assigned to him..." (ESV)

This chapter refers to the unmistakable fact that as believers not only receive eternal life, but also the abundant life when looking in scripture by Christ.We will explore the life alternating truth that we can experience a life of adundance when we sacrifice to God.

When we are in our element, or spiritual gift, there is nothing more addicting than what we are experiencing. We were made for this. This is our bread and butter. Our storming the Bastille. Our Normandy. This, the gift we have been given, is awesome to take in and watch. Especially in another person

I watched Martha oooz the Gospel. It ran through her veins. She breathed Christ. This was part of her journey. We are so much conditioned to concentrate on the destination that we forget that "life is a journey not a destination." (Unknown) Take a look at this quote. It has some sage advice in it.

How do you know if an animal is alive or dead. Well, one way is to see if the animal has stopped breathing. Another way is if there is blood. There is life in the blood. During the time of Christ the sacrificial lamb was an offering of the Isrealites to God. This slain lamb was life to the ones who slain the lamb. There was redemption in the blood of the lamb. Jesus was called the Lamb of God. Jesus was ticket to eternal life. His blood covered us in the same way the Israelites painted the blood of a lamb on the door of the household. The angel of death would pass over the house who had the blood on its' door frame. Thus, He is our Passover lamb. He sacrificd Himself and became our Passover lamb. There is life in His shed blood for us. Does it get any better than this? Talk about sacrifice. It is not confined to the Old Testament, but there are people today who will lay down his/her life for another. Just look at Martha, my prayer partner. When faced with unfathomable choices she choose life. The life inside her. Chemo and radiation. She gave her body to Christ. Again. Only now there was life inside her. Bad luck. I think not. It was all God plan. Why I will never understand. But I trust God. When all else fails Martha had to trust God with His divine plan. His ways are higher than our way. So Martha was obedient to God. She laid down her life for her daughter. Is there a greater love than that? On earth I mean.

Then there was a man called Jesus who laid down His life for you and me. It is what I call sacrificial love. Same with Martha. She was in His hands. I have never seen something like this so beautiful. He had Martha in the palm of His hand. She was obedient when most women would have opted to save their own lives. Martha gave her body up to Him to do as He pleased. Only Martha could have carried a miracle in her body for 8 months and delivered a 100% healthy baby girl. Chemo and radiation and all. God choose to call Martha home a few months after the miracle birth. Why I do not know. I will never know or understand His divine plan. But hey He is God, not me. I have to remind myself of this several times a day.

Her sacrifice filled me up like nothing else. Just like Mary of Bethany poured out the pure nard on Jesus. She sacrificed a year's wages on this perfume. Everyone got onto her.Gave her grief. She "wasted" it on Christ. Did He agree? Oh no. He called her sacrifice beautiful in the Word. She had a tender heart. She was devoted to Christ. She loved Him immensely. Before Martha died she told me to move on and to make friends. She knew this would not be easy for me. She told me I had a tender heart. She knew I might get stuck in the muck and mire of grief. She knew me all too well. She told me to move on with life. It was a sobering visit. Would I trust her or go on in the abyss of the upcoming grief? This song got me through the abyss. I had a choice, to trust God or else stay in the death pit.

Look at the following verse on life and what you must have to live:

> Exodus 12:13 "The blood shall be a sign for you, on the houses where you are. And when I see the blood, I will pass over you..." (ESV)

Thus God passes over the households not because they put a sign the front yard, For Sale by Owner, or because Mom and Dad had college educated children, or they had a certain income no, the angel of death passed over becaue of the blood of an animal that was sacrificed and its blood was painted on their door frames. Sound familiar? It should. Jesus because of his shed blood on thre cross, made God the Father pass over the believers and not kill their first born.because of the blood on the door frame. There is power in the blood of Christ. It was a matter of life or death for the children of Isreal. Life is blood. Life in sacrifice. Sounds like a momma I introduced you to in this book. Without blood there is no life. That sacrificial love for us was him giving up his body for us to live. Martha gave up her body to Christ so that the life inside her could live. One life for another life. Sounds like the ultimate sacrifice to me. Martha knew whose she was and that He would work it all out for His good and perfect ways. That is where I adamantly disagree or don't understand it is a better word for it.

Look at the following verses. Which one do you like the best?

Exodus 12:13 "The blood will be a sign for you, over the houses where you are,. and when I see the blood, I will pass over you, and no plague will befall you to destroy you, when I strike the land of Egypt."(ESV)

Hewbrews 13:12 " So Jesus also suffered outside the gate in order to sanctify the people through his own blood."(ESV)

1John 1:7b "..and the blood of Jesus His Son cleaneses us from all sin." (ESV)

What is the common denominator in all these verses? Blood, pure and simple. There is life in the blood. That is true of every human and animal who has ever graced this planet or was ever born. That leads us to another point. Jesus' conception and birth was the only exception to that rule. The immaculate conception it is called. The virgin Mary. The only woman who never had sex and yet gave birth. Behold the Lambof God. Born of a human mother. Heaven Sent. Why on eath would He, surrounded by the myriads of saying"Holy holy holy" leave perfection in heaven? . The all you can eat buffett. That includes the all you cn eat buffett; fahitas, and queso dip. I cannot for the life of me understand that kind of love. God became a man so he could not merely sympathize with us but rather to say I understnd and sympathize with us. A real Savior with real human needs and therefore feel the emotions we feel. It blows my mind. How about you?

Christ gave up everything for us. The all you can eat buffet, the angels circuling the throne saying, Holy, holy, holy, the casting of crowns at His feet. What is it that God wants from us? Simply-put. He wants us. All of us. Check out the lyrics to this song.

I use to think when I was little that if I carried my Bible to church and was a good person, attended church and was nice for the most part that I was heaven bound. It wasn't until our youth director had something that I wanted. There was just something about her made me want what she had. What made her tick?

I remember very distinctly when I was a junior in high school what my youth director said. She said to have eternal life that you had to ask Christ to come into your life or heart. Christ, she said, was a gentleman and that He would not go where He wasn't invited.She went onto another job and school but I never forgot what she said. It took me four years to finally ask Christ into my life. But I did. I call it the restroom revival. I didn't know the sinner's prayer. I said these simple words...Jesus come inside me. That was it. I was a born again believer. It was that simple. But oh, the results were immediate. I accepted Christ on the way to the restroom.Thus, my restroom revival.

The most visable way I had become a Christian was that I stopped cheating in school. Sad but true. I figured that if I let Christ in me that He deserved to have every part of me. That included school. My friends were shocked. Yup, I was changing my ways. Or rather, Christ was changing my ways.

The biggest blessing I have ever received was and is my daughter. We were married for 9 years before she came along. She is such a joy and blessing to me. Although she is an adult now, she will always be the joy of my life. I received that blessing from the good Lord above. Each day that I have her I am thankful to God. She is so loving, smart, forgiving, and an overall an awesome daughter. It is suffix to say I love her beyong these words. I am truly blessed.

The biggest gift we have is life. If you have ever been very ill, you know first hand how precious life is. None of us is not guaranteed another day here on planet earth. While some people think they are entitled to their right to abort the life inside them, I respectually disagree.The two Godliest women I know had abortions early on in their adult life. If ever a gal had the right to a medically necessary abortion it was Martha. She told me it was an easy choice. No abortion, rather, chemo and all while pregnant. It was a child not a choice. What a legacy Martha's daughter has.

A mother who choose her at all cost. Now that is love. Born of a mother's love. That was my best friend. My prayer partner. How much she loved and was glad to see her daughter when she was born. It had been a long pregnancy to say the least. It all melted away she said when she heard and saw her daughter for the first time.

Chapter 8

Receiving Grace

Jeremiah 31:2a ..."found grace in the wilderness."
(ESV)

Whenever God's children sacrifice great gifts to Him, He provides enough grace suffiecent to finish the task. By viewing both women in this book, readers will be comforted that each of us is capable of making it through extremely difficult circumstances via grace from The Father.

God says in scripture that we are to be "perfect as as our heavenly Father is perfect."(Matthew 5:48, ESV) What you may question? How on earth can I be perfect. It is impossible. You are dead right. We aren't but Christ is. When we accep tChrist into our lives then God the Father looks at our heart he does not see all the muck and mire ofour lives and sin, He sees the perfection of Christ. And His perfect sacrifice for our sins and declaers us not guilty.If not, then we won't enjoy the all you caneat buffet upstairs!!!

God loves us too much to leave us to our own devices.Will we have trials? Without adoubt we will. It is called the sanctification process. Just like the blacksmith uses fire to mold his object into a beautiful object. God says we too are being molded into what

He wants us to become. Check out this verse which confirms this thinking.

> 1Peter 1:6b-7..."you have been grieved by various trials, so that the tested genuineness of your raith more precious than gold that perishes through it is tested by fire..."(ESV)

It is absurb to thinkwe will get everything we pray for. Some believers are dupped into thinking God is a Coke machine. In goes the prayer or quarter and out comes the answered prayer we desire and out comes the desired product, a Coke. God answers prayers in three ways; yes, no, or wait. I highly suggest you keep a prayer journal with request. Put on one the date of request and the request and when it is answered. Some requests will be immediate. Some may take many

May take many years I had took 6 years till I saw an anser. This will revolutionize your prayer life. It is exciting and devasating all at once. Although we cannot see God's hand in the immediate, it may take many, many years to come to fruition. Some we will never see in this lifetime.Those are the facts mam. God is not a coke machine.

All I know is that at the time Martha died, I had no best firnd. Now twenty years later I have so many friends, I don't know what to do with all of them!. I thought I would never have a best friend again. Enter God. Now I have many best friends. Who would have thought that then? God was refining me.See what I wrote almost almost twenty years ago.

Earlier I quoted Jerimiah said he "found grace in the wilderness." (Jerimiah 31:2a ESV). Sometimes during our dark days we cling to Christ more than anything else. Perhaps that is because we have exhausted all other means. Sometimes God allows us to wander in the wilderness so we will hear us while speaking, or alas, shouting to us. It is in this dark place that we are left with no choice to listen to Him.

That was the case with Martha. At one point Martha had slipped into a coma and was a death's door. She was in ICU. I was let in by her husband. What do I do? What do I say to her? I sang our favorite song…"I love you Lord and I lift my voice, to worship you O my soul rejoice, take joy my king in what you hear, may it be a sweet sweet song in your ear." (by Lauriee Klein) I sang it two or three times and then Martha squeezed my hand. A coincidence? I think not. She was still there and with us. She was not being called home that night.

Which takes us to Mary of Bethany. She did something that irritated the disciples and clergy. He hung out with sinners. The low lifes. The scum of the earth. And then there was Mary who anointed Jesus for His burial. Mary, Martha, and Lazarus was Him oasis in the desert. They were His support team. I firmly believe they knew He was living on borrowed time. They somehow knew, especially Mary,that the cross lie ahead. Why else would Mary anoint Him? She knew. I am sure of that. But the others, I am not sure of.

Below are some quotes on grace. Which one is your favorite? Why?

What has been your favorite quote? Why?

Chapter 9

Receiving Peace

Philippians 4:19

"And the peace of God which surpasses all understanding, will guard your hearts and minds in Christ Jesus." (ESV)

This chapter is devoted to the unsurpassing peace that comes from sacrifice. Both peace that comes from sacrifice. Both women experienced peace behond measure after very public acts of obedience of love for their maker.

Hold onto your hat, we are about to look at six scripture verses. Ready Verne?

Ephesians 2:14a "For he himself is our peace..."(ESV)

John14:27a "Peace I leave you; my peace I give to you. Not as the world gives do I give to you."(ESV)

Colossians 1:20b ....making peace by the blood of his cross."(ESV)

> Romans 5:1 "Therefore, since we have been justified by faith, we have peace with God through our Lord Jesus Christ." (ESV)

> Isaiah 26:3 "You keep him in peace whose mind is stayed on you because he trusts in you."

Peace is all elusive. At least I think so. I watched our youth director for over four years and could not put my finger on what she had until she shared the Gospel with us junior high and senior high students at church. It was not the eternal life that drew me to Christ, it wasn't the forgiveness that drew me to Him. What in the world did Debbie? It was the peace that He brought to the table. My life was such a roller coaster that I did not like the up and downs of it. Tennis may have had something to do with it. Although I was ranked #1 in my state I was still not satisfied with my life. It was so up and down. Emotions running the gamet. It was not until I was a junior that I said, "please come inside me." No theology. No right or wrong way to do it. I believe it was that simple. From then on I tried to live for Him. In everything. School and tennis and yes, even dating. I got born again. And finally I got some peace. I could rest my head on my pillow and take a big sigh and say, "it is ok, I'm ok." Peace was the byproduct of my relationship with Christ. I felt like a new person. "Therefore, if anyone is in Christ, he is a new creation. The old has passed away; behold, the new has come." 2 Corinthians 5:17, (ESV)

The last time I ever saw Martha alive was on a Thursday in mid November. She was weak and didn't talk that much. She motioned for me to get closer to her as she was about to tell me something important.

"Debbie, I am going to die soon. Promise me one thing."

"Anything in the world" I said.

"Promise me that you will not mourn me too long and when my husband remarries soon, that you will welcome his new wife into your life."

Oh, so easy to say and yet so hard to do.

Whenever I played tennis I use to get so nervous and played nervous until the match was over. I never felt at ease or at peace. You wouldn't know it by looking at me. During practice I was totally at ease or peace. Never nervous playing someone in private sets. But competition was a different thing all together. I use to say Philippians 4:13 :"I can do all things through him who strengthens me." (ESV) over and over throughout the match. It was my peace. He was my peace.

When I ran the marathon for Martha's memory I said this verse over and over again...all 26.2 miles. It became my mantra. It helped get some peace from Martha's death. I was trying to somehow keep her memory alive. I like to think she was looking down at me and smiling. I know in my heart that God gave her a glimpse of my dedication of the marathon to her. At least in my book she was looking. I found my peace that day. In Him, and in her life she lived for Him.

I think we were pretty good prayer partners. She was what is called "a keeper."

Would you be able to find peace in a son's or daughter's death? How about in a spouse's death. A sudden death like a car accident or a slow illness such as cancer? It is not peace in the circumstance we are looking for. For we cannot change fate. But rather it is a peace, God's peace, that we look for in all situations we face on a daily basis. I don't know about you but I need peace each and every day. I never found it in tennis. Not one time. I was always so nervous, no matter who I was playing or where I was playing. I had butterflies in my tummy the whole time I stepped on the court. Sad but true

But when I was around other believers I was at peace. Why was that? I think when we are around other Christians we are at peace. Maybe not. May on the beach is our solace. Maybe church. Maybe in your car singing loudly with the windows rolled up, maybe at school. Wherever your safe place is be sure of this...God is with you. Wherever you hang your hat, He is there. And here's the kicker. He been with you throughout your life. In every situation. In every dark corridor you go down. He is with you through the good, bad, and ugly. Perhaps you were like me. It is not until we give Him our lives that we can tap into the elusive peace. But it is there for us at all times. He knows the exact moment we become a believer and He knows all we want is peace. His sacrifice is there for us. He is out peace. I love it that He is called The Prince of Peace. You'd think He knows our struggles and pain. It is called empathy. He became so poor at that stable so we could be lavished at the foot of the cross. He is our peace. Let's don't every forget it.

Chapter 10

Receiving the Fullness of Christ

Job 23:14a

"For he will complete what he appoints for me.."
(ESV)

This book ends by taking a look at the fullness each of us can have when we enter into a sacrificial relationship with Christ. While each of us gives in different ways to God, each gift is radical when given out of love and devotion to Him.

Check out these awesome verses on the fullness of Christ. Be sure and choose your favorite

John 1:16 "And from his fullness we have all received grace upon grace.: (ESV)

Ephesians 4:13" ...which is his body, the fullnesss of him who fills all in all."(ESV)

Colossians 1:19 "For in him all; the fullness of God was pleased to dwell." (ESV)

John 1;14 "And the Word became flesh and dwelt among us, and we have seen his glory, glory as of the only Son from the father full of grace and truth."(ESV)

When Adam and Eve lost perfection that fateful day in the Garden of Eden, we were conceived in sin in our mother's womb. What was secretly stolen in the Garden would one day have to be bought back publically at the Cross. When you and I accept Christ or decide to follow Him the rest of our lives, we have with us the fullness of Christ and all the "fringe benefits" with Him.

What is receiving the fullness of God? It is quite simply trusting in Him and taking back from Satan all the things that ours were long long ago. Actually we have those things instantly when we give our lives to Christ. But somewhere in the muck and mire of life, we forget that it has already been given to us. What is our part of the salvation experience? Quite simply, we sin. What Deb? You must be joking? That's predestation isn't it? All I know is this: Apart from Christ we can do nothing." (John 5a)

I use to struggle about wherther or not Muslims, Jews, or new agers got to heaven or not. What if they aren't told of Christ in the Congo? What about babies and todldlers that die? There is an age of accoubbntability, thank the good Lord. All I know after all these years is this…God is in control, not me. I just trust him to sort that all out. Not me. I have a heard time with it. But I don't worry about it becausue as Twila Praris wrote, God is in control. Let's look at her incredible song.

When we accept Christ into our lives we automatically receive all the fullness in Him. We are given certain spiritual gifts and He also reveals to us, if we will listen, other gifts as well. Gifts are usually ones that we enjoy, not hate. For example, although I was not a believer when I was ten years old, I still loved to wtite poetry. I even entered the 4th grade talent contest. I wrote a poem that I still know by heart. It is the following. Don't laugh too hard.

Morning Dew
By Debbie Vanderslice

The fresh morning dew slowly slid up my shoe,
I wondered a while
As it added up into a pile

My teacher asked about my shoe
I told her it got wet in the fresh
morning dew

(1979)

What gift or gifts has God given you? You may blush and hem haw around and say, "Oh, I don't have any that I know of."

I emphatically disagree. If you are a believer you have been bestowed with certain spiritual gifts. Are you still wondering what yours is? When you do it or see it you will know.

Martha's time was almost up. I remember the night she died. It was in mid to late November when she passed away. I dreaded the call that came around 11pm. It snowed that night. I felt as though God was saying, "She lived a pure life for me. Just like this snow is pure, so was she." At least I felt that was what God was saying to me.

It has been a long jouney for both you and I. I think you will agree that my friend, Martha gave the ultimate gift of all. Life. I know she was not going to have it any other way. She was stubborn that way. I found her once after a chemo round on top of a chair painting a mural in her daughter's room.

I told Martha to get down off that chair. She just laughed. She said what's going to happen to me? I fall and die? You kinda needed to be there to get the full effect. Martha had accepted her lot in life and was not bitter at all. Unlike me, who had stopped talking to God altogether. I heard her say on many occasions…"I know I am terminal. But you don't know when your time is. You are the one

I feel sorry for. Don't feel sorry for me, feel badly about the people who are going to be left behind. Those are the ones who will be in pain. Me? I will have no pain and am going to a perfect place. It is all part of the jouney. My journey."

And so we are at the end of the road. I learned what life and death sacrifice was all about. I had a front row seat. I won't lie, it was painful and addicting all at the same time. Mary in scriptures broke the jar of pure nard/perfume and anointed Christ. It was her very personal and best gift she could give Christ before He was to go to the cross. Likewise, my friend Martha gave up her body to Christ as a living sacrifice. She obeyed the Word and I saw Christ flow through her in a way I never have before. I know she is in heaven cheering me on as is Jesus. Both were an oasis to this believer. And the house was filled with the perfume...how sweet it it is. How sweet it is.

Printed in the United States
By Bookmasters